To Whom It May Concern

Edited by

Becki Mee

First published in Great Britain in 1999 by
POETRY NOW
Remus House, Coltsfoot Drive, Woodston,
Peterborough, PE2 9JX
Telephone (01733) 898101
Fax (01733) 313524

All Rights Reserved

Copyright Contributors 1999

HB ISBN 0 75430 608 9
SB ISBN 0 75430 609 7

Foreword

Although we are a nation of poetry writers we are accused of not reading poetry and not buying poetry books: after many years of listening to the incessant gripes of poetry publishers, I can only assume that the books they publish, in general, are books that most people do not want to read.

Poetry should not be obscure, introverted, and as cryptic as a crossword puzzle: it is the poet's duty to reach out and embrace the world.

The world owes the poet nothing and we should not be expected to dig and delve into a rambling discourse searching for some inner meaning.

The reason we write poetry (and almost all of us do) is because we want to communicate: an ideal; an idea; or a specific feeling. Poetry is as essential in communication, as a letter; a radio; a telephone, and the main criteria for selecting the poems in this anthology is very simple: they communicate.

CONTENTS

Title	Author	Page
Drunk And A Bottle	Amanda Gidding	1
The Traveller	Alan Compton	2
Baby Belief	Lawrance-Marc Richards	3
Message In A Bottle	B R Lloyd	4
Message In A Bottle	Simon Peter Dennis	5
The Castaway	Ian Fowler	6
Beyond The Horizon	Pippa Lovell	7
Galleons	Norman Royal	8
Lost At Sea	A K S Shaw	9
Lost Soul	Amanda S Holland	10
Chain Letter	Maria-Christina	11
My Last Hope	Alexina Reid Whyte	12
Thank God It's Friday!	Peter Davies	13
A Bottle Of Hope	Margaret Andrews	14
Time And Space	Evelyn Annies	15
Alien Alert	Lorna Lea	16
Message In A Bottle	Shaun Turner	17
Message In A Bottle	Ghazanfer Eqbal	18
Drifting Poetry	Phillip A Taylor	19
Tell The People	Patrick Kelly	20
From The Sea, With The Fog, They Roll In!	Philip Trivett	21
Solitude	Maureen Watson	22
God's Message	Mary Skelton	23
Message In A Bottle	Joan Jones	24
Message In A Bottle	Nicki Cornwell	25
Distant Dream	Ruth Daviat	26
Troubled Sea	Simon Barjona	27
All In The Mind	Dorothy Whitehall	28
Never Heard	S Mullinger	29
Regrets	Arlyn Harry Navis	30
Wendy Island Bay	Peter James O'Rourke	31
The Legacy	Amanda-Lea Manning	32
Message In A Bottle 1	June M Bootle	34

For My Love	Carol Rickard	35
The Parents' Precedent	Gillian C Fisher	36
Message In A Bottle	Pauline Uprichard	37
A Bottle Swimming Near	Emma Freeman	38
All Washed Up	B C Watts	39
Island 20' 72"	Fiona Bower	40
To Whoever	Elizabeth Dobie	41
Send Out Sustenance/SOS	F B Broomfield	42
Our Bottled Message	G D Eccleston	44
Hi!	J M Service	45
Message In A Bottle	Lynda Margaret Fitch	46
Message In A Bottle	Tracy Bell	47
Leaving School	Anne Sanderson	48
A Reptilian Scene	Alistair McLean	49
Whispers Of The Sea	A Richards	50
She Had To Go	Frieda Cox	52
The Bottle	Dusty Sutherland	53
Returned To Sender	Wenn The Penn	54
A Bottle Of Hope	Paul Gold	55
The Bottled Note	Robert Wassell	56
My Message	Louisa Gibb	57
All Washed Up!	Joyce Hockley	58
Timely Warning	Grace Mills	59
Single Lens Reflex	Robert D Shooter	60
And!	Graham Mitchell	61
Message In A Bottle	Betty Green	62
A Message To Whomever	R J Chapman	63
Mushroom	K M Clemo	64
Bottle Message	Alma Montgomery Frank	65
I Myself	Evelyn Balmain	66
Pandora's Bottle	R L Cooper	67
Someone Somewhere	Peter Fordham	68
The Human Race	Chrissi	70
Alone In A Bottle	Sylvia Ranby	71
Message In A Bottle	J Mary Kirkland	72
If Anyone	Keith L Powell	73

The Love Bottle	Paddy Jupp	74
Around Forever	Susan Timmis	75
What's The Weather Like?	Linda J Clarke	76
Second-Glass Post	Maureen Atkin	77
Bottled Message	Jack Judd	78
Mind In A Bottle	C O Burnell	79
Message In A Bottle	Brian Willis	80
My Message In A Bottle	Merilyn Gulley	81
Help	Joy Benford	82
Freedom!	Dancer	83
Titanic	Sunny Gunessee	84
Shipwrecked	Robert McCall	85
Message In A Bottle	Helena Edwards Bishop	86
RSVP	Barbara L Richards	87
Message In A Bottle	Phoenix Martin	88
Seaworthy?	Elizabeth Mark	89
Sonnet: Bright Eyes Burning Like Fire	J D Winchester	90
Listen!	Annemarie Poole	91
Message In A Bottle	F Jensen	92
Guilty	Bob Wydell	93
Out Of Reach	Colin Allsop	94
To Who It May Concern	Coleen Bradshaw	95
A World Alone	Esme Francis	96
A Message In A Bottle	A Jessop	97
I Wonder	B M Hurll	98
Message In A Bottle	Elizabeth Cowley Guscott	99
To A Stranger	Joyce Pompei	100
Before Words	Dan Pugh	101
Message In A Bottle	Leonard Coleman	102
A Wish Within	B G Clarke	104
The Last Resort	Roger Williams	105
River	K J Seeley	106
Bottle-Chart Omission	Hilary Jill Robson	107
Tricky Treasure	C Shadwell	108
Message In A Bottle	Renie Calcraft	109

Please Listen	Joan Lister	110
Message In A Bottle	Elaine Beresford	111
Message Of Hope	Alister H Thomson	112
Green, Opaque And Tantalising	Helen Perry	113
Beached Bottles	Kim Montia	114
Waves Of Change	Clive Cornwall	115
A Forethought	Margaret Gleeson Spanos	116
Enigma	Linda Anne Landers	117
Send Someone Please	Maxine Beck	118
From Bandos Island	Sue Knight	119

DRUNK AND A BOTTLE

After I watched you sail away,
I really wished I'd asked you to stay,
The sails disappeared, the horizon was blank,
With tears in my eyes, my heavy heart sank.

What of the things that I should have said,
Wouldn't leave my mouth; just stayed in my head,
What can I do now, I've left it too late,
A sad goodbye that was our last date.

I then returned home with a bottle of wine,
Drinking and hoping that things would be fine,
I stood up and swayed, it was nearly a topple,
Wine induced brainwave, I'll make use of the bottle.

I wrote all my feelings, a large piece of paper,
Knowing it's stupid, a drunk's desperate caper,
Now holding the bottle crammed with the facts,
I kissed it and corked it and sealed it with wax.

Dropped in the water on an outgoing tide,
I felt myself smile when I could have cried,
It made me feel better, I'd filled a big space,
Thinking one day it might reach the right place.

I'll never forget that unfortunate day,
When I'd written down all I wanted to say,
The message disappeared, the horizon was blank,
For all I knew the wine bottle sank!

Amanda Giddings

THE TRAVELLER

It's good to be home in England again
After months in sunnier lands
Where the raucous, unmelodic screech
Of birds rends the listless air:
Where the sun bores down with relentless
Force, and one longs for the night's release.

Yes, it's good to walk in the woods again
To the sound of sweeter songs
And the fragrant smell of new-mown
Grass on the gentle, soft summer breeze:
Where a robin hop-hops along the path
With cheeky, fearless glance,
And a squirrel scampers for cover
And curious, peeps round the bole of a tree.
Yes it's good to be home.

Alan Compton

BABY BELIEF

The sun slips from the sky and the Earth heavily cries
for all its children no longer able to see.
Yet we are strong to know we are weak
and our arms shall lift us up
when we can no longer carry this weight.
For in these dark dank days of blind faith
no burden will break such backs bent so straight.

Aeons have passed throughout our veins
in waters of time and unknown soldiers
wearily within our skin.
Yet still we strain to peel free laden lids
and open life's delicate vapour sealed inside our being.

If we were mountains we'd be scaled to hills
where ramblers and pylons would mark us still.
But we're more the air of gravity and inertia
giving birth to our child to continue our cycle.

Lawrance-Marc Richards

MESSAGE IN A BOTTLE
(Where Are You Now?)

To whoever finds this bottle green
However far away your land,
Please send a reply as I am keen
To know how fate has played her hand.

Is your country an exotic place?
An island lush with trees and flowers,
With crystal streams gushing down cliff face
And golden sands and leafy bowers.
Or is it a desert arid and hot.

Maybe an oasis where all can drink.
Camels and Arabs mill about a lot?
Perhaps you live in a city, I think,
Where skyscrapers tower over people small.
There are theatres, cinemas as well
And families shop in the shopping mall.

Wherever you live please write and tell
If any of my dreams are true.
Or if this is nothing like your place
Will be pleased to hear about you
Perhaps one day I'll be allowed to see your mystery face.

B R Lloyd

MESSAGE IN A BOTTLE

The year I believe is 1912
Read in what you can to this I delve
I boarded the Titanic for its maiden voyage
Me and my mate, my mate called Noyage
We were going to America to claim our fame
But the distance between was enough to make our name
On this ship what happened
Nobody thought of this while there was joy in the wind
Unsinkable RMS Titanic
But when we hit that iceberg the was mass panic
This was the captain's very last cruise
He wanted to go out in style and wanted to make the news
Reporters were interested and wanted to make their own name
Gain that recognition and even fame
But what developed on that crispy cold night
In the North Atlantic it carried enough bite
When the Titanic ship finally went down
The scenes were petrifying and you heard the sounds
The sounds of anguish pain and fear
It was no way to go but I love you my dear
They were my last words I said to my wife
I had to leave her, take on board this strife
She boarded the boat no room for men
All I can say is and then Den
They sent us to be demoralised
The events got worse as the cold gripped your eyes
Panic set in so did the *ice*
Not enough boats, thousands paid the price
The water was so cold it just froze you
Pure pandemonium, nothing you could do.

Simon Peter Dennis

The Castaway

Whoever has received this bottle
Please write back to me
For this is why I placed
This message in the sea.

I haven't spoken to anyone
In many a long year
I often look around but
No one ever comes near.

I don't know exactly
How I ended up this way
Everything was going great
Until that frightful day.

Was I deserted by a ship
Or washed upon the shore
I guess it has never really
Mattered all that much before.

But may I just inform you
Before you return my note
That it would be advisable
To get yourself a boat.

You see I am marooned on an island
In the middle of the sea
That is why your reply
Is so important to me.

Ian Fowler

BEYOND THE HORIZON

This message I bring
On the crest of a wave,
A special bottle
Recycled and saved.

The sea had an inviting glow
A short time ago.
Water, warm, sensuous and clear,
At present, pollution I fear.

Bad conditions I now can see,
Industrial waste, sewage and algae.
Fish and molluscs washed up on the shore,
Starved of oxygen, they could take no more.

Newspapers and magazines,
Are a help it seems.
Discussions about polluting our sea,
With waste from our lavatories.

If we carry on the way we are,
Abusing and disrupting the sea,
There will be nothing left,
For our children and families.

Pippa Lovell

GALLEONS

Galleons in the lemon light
Crossing seas of blue,
Worlds across the billowing sky
Which one tonight is mine?

Seen you in your boats of play
Treasures upon the moon,
Felt your clouds of silken charm
Around the suns of rhyme.

Going to sail to Saturn
Catch the morning's breeze,
Turn the bands of gold around
To meet the missing stream.

Wild hair blowing over bridges
Takes the time to sing,
Soft kisses over ocean's calm
Into bays of harbour's wine.

Jasmine jars of slow unwinding scent
From far Eastern lands of plenty,
Escape to catch the evening's shine
To turn the tides of dream.

Norman Royal

LOST AT SEA

Without your love I'm lost and all at sea,
Drifting single-handed, lonely, petrified,
Wondering if you still remember me.

I've sailed my wayward course despondently,
As indecisive as the changing tide,
Without your love my mind is all at sea.

You got away with everything scot-free.
No maintenance, no lawyer by my side.
You could at least sometimes remember me.

My looks are gone, your infidelity
Has pierced my tender heart, and crushed my pride.
Without your love my life is all at sea.

And while that hipless whore, your wife to be,
Clings like a limpet, dumb and starry-eyed,
You'll see no reason to remember me.

Goodbye, you cheat, for all eternity.
This final note shall bridge the great divide.
'Without your love this day I drowned at sea.
This bottled hand is mine. *Remember* me'.

A K S Shaw

LOST SOUL

A kindred spirit hear my plea,
Alone and lost, suffering like me,
Endless days, a dark auspicious night,
Answer my call and end my plight.

For many years, I have roamed this isle,
No other soul do I beguile,
Lost in my thoughts, memories abound,
Answer my calls, hear my sound.

From the shore I await, to hear you reply,
Do not leave me here to suffer and cry,
Wave of hope, an answer I implore,
To you my soul-mate, I will open my door.

Amanda S Holland

CHAIN LETTER

Dear brother or sister,
When you find this message:

Please make copies and
Pass on to others
With a request in turn
To pass on this message
Of friendship and peace.

I send you my love
In this 'empty' bottle.
Love increases when given away
So when you have done this
Please reseal the bottle
And return it to the sea.
So shall we spread around the world
The message of peace and joy and goodwill
In ever-widening ripples.

May this chain letter
So unite people of goodwill,
Of every race, colour and creed
That the world will become one nation and
War, prejudice and hatred will be no more.

Maria-Christina

MY LAST HOPE

I'm praying that someone out there
Will find this bottle in the sea
I'm marooned on an island.
There is no one else but me.

One time I'm on a world cruise,
then I'm overboard,
I don't know how I'm still alive,
I can only thank the Lord.

I'm praying that you find me
Before it is too late.
I've been living off the island
Anything edible I've ate.

I'm praying for a miracle,
That someone swimming in the sea,
Will find this message in the bottle,
And send a ship to rescue me.

Alexina Reid Whyte

THANK GOD IT'S FRIDAY!

I'm on a desert island,
I'm as frightened as can be,
I hope you heed my message,
And come and rescue me.

I've been here for a lifetime,
Please save me someone quick,
You'll find my wife in Croydon
She must be worried sick!

There's someone here beside me,
And 'though it sounds absurd,
She is a blonde with ruby lips
Who doesn't say a word.

We've tried to get attention,
From many a passing craft.
But on they go regardless,
They think we must be daft!

I'll never see my family,
I'll die of thirst and heat,
For I'm on a traffic island
In the midst of Oxford Street!

Peter Davies

A Bottle Of Hope

Dear Reader, I hope this message reaches you dry and clear -
For it has in it many important things which I would like you to hear,
I wrote in ball-pointed pen just in case the lid should go amiss
Hoping it will reach you, I admit I'm taking a mighty risk.

Do you think that we could meet up and make plans to
    change the world?
To make decent beings of every man, woman, boy and girl?
To make the sun shine instead of having heavy downpours
    of torturous rain?
To bring some cheer and ease the great pain?

Do you think that we could still keep the dream alive of
    living in harmony and peace?
Protect the vulnerable who live on all five continents surrounded
    by the beautiful sea?
Wipe the tears from the suffering and the forlorn
And pray in the night for a brighter future when we awaken
    in the morn?

If this message reached you will you promise to make a difference
    to somebody's life?
May he be a poor man, a sad youth or an embittered wife?
Reach out and touch the needy of this world instead of sitting
    idly at home?
Somebody out there needs you - is bereft and so alone.

If rocks do not break my bottle and the paper I write on is not
    eaten by a fish or whale -
And if it is not blown away by an almighty gale,
Will you please help in whichever way you can?
But if you don't reply I'll know that it hadn't reached you -
    never made its way to dry land.

Margaret Andrews

TIME AND SPACE

Time is man-made did you know
It used not to exist
If we went back 2000 years
Time would not be missed.
Man uses it to pace himself
And build his world upon
Me thinks he's getting far too clever
And someday will go wrong.

People call it progress
But when all is said and done
Things are there to be discovered
Nothing is new under the sun
Man will bring about his own destruction
The Bible tells us so
Trouble is it may be sooner
Than we want to go.

If we could turn the clock back
To save some money's worth
That money could be spent to help our people
Who are starving here on earth.
Of course it's very clever
Sending rockets out in space
But no one will ever live there
Well, not the human race!

The air is non-existent
Even if we could fly
To live there would be impossible
First we have to die.

Evelyn Annies

ALIEN ALERT

Alien, alert . . . attention, attention,
Earth's in danger of destruction.

Message here in bottle,
Planet in distress.
I must tell the finder,
Our world is in a mess.

Reader of this missive,
We're running out of hope.
Maybe you can help us,
And show us how to cope.

Disregard this Mayday,
And we will surely die.
Inscribe a panacea,
Right across our sky.

Return immediate answer,
Make us understand
The process of reversal,
So we can save our land.

Teach us, from your knowledge,
How to stop pollution,
We need to save farm animals
From savage execution.

Forewarn meagre Earthlings,
Of penalties of drugs.
Show our scientists methods
Of controlling super bugs.

Send us fast instructions
How to seal the ozone hole,
To stay the ice caps melting,
And make peace on Earth our goal.

Lorna Lea

MESSAGE IN A BOTTLE

Excuse me girl for thinking
that I was being polite,
but this boat won't stop sinking
and I'm holding on tight -
Don't let my temperature stop me,
from being right, but if we don't
leave a message, we'll be bottled
up for life.
We said 'Hello island,' as we
sailed into the day. Leaving a
message, like the man from
Milk Tray. The polite message
did reach, all the sailors, but
then again this island was
Pennsylvania.
All messages for sailors were getting
to decline, but keep in touch with it
and your life, will be designed.
As the message suddenly multiplied
in value to the sailors. Everybody
wanted to go, to old Pennsylvania.
We relied on each other, to live after
death and the feeling, for each other,
as we controlled every breath - and
the feelings just sailed in the
Pennsylvania heat.
The message in a bottle, always
let it speak. We sailed away to
a land in open arms, so let
everybody be happy and calm, to a
different world saying hello. There
is no harm in laying a message
in a bottle you know.

Shaun Turner

MESSAGE IN A BOTTLE
(Dedicated to Afifa and Fahad)

It is a message in a bottle
have we not hit the goal . . . the target
you might have seen a picture
or read in a book
Messages sent in a bottle
to find a loved one
or to be responded and reciprocated
to reach the sender of the message
or the imitation of the message
it was exactly like this
when I first saw you
wondering . . . wandering
whether my love will reach you.
coax you cajole you then and there
spontaneously . . . instantly . . . intuitively, instinctively.
I admit, I accept I love you
you . . . you . . . lovely . . . lovely . . . love you
in need of you to make a nest
to live and look after each other
by one another for procreating
creating a symbol of our love
lovely love . . . loving love . . . love . . . forever.

Ghazanfer Eqbal

DRIFTING POETRY

If you find this bottle
And the message it does hold
Then riddle and rhyme of a bygone time
Shall before your eyes unfold.

And when you find the answer
And this you shall find
My name and my passion
Is the reward for your time

Find a book by Anchor
Seek a poem called 'The Kiss'
Read it very carefully
Not a line should you miss.

It will teach you to be patient
Passionate and kind
You will then find the publishers
Who will give you my name in kind.

Phillip A Taylor

TELL THE PEOPLE

Oppression, depression stop the folk from progression
    'Universal Message'.
    'Universal Lesson'.

Good things happen with social communication,
    'Universal Understanding'.
    'Universal Celebration'.

Sunshine from blue heaven above,
    'Universal Peace'.
    'Universal Love'.

Patrick Kelly

FROM THE SEA, WITH THE FOG, THEY ROLL IN!

'Hello, what's this?'

I thought as I strolled along the Cornish beach.
A bottle floating in a rock pool,
I climbed over to get it, for it was just in my reach.
There's some paper, let's see what message is within . . .

'Stay clear! Do you hear?
Don't dare come near.
We've a very serious situation here.
If you find this message, run for your lives.
Arm yourselves with anything; guns, clubs or knives!
Don't go alone, travel in packs no fewer than five.
Then at least there's a chance of one of you getting out alive!

'They're here on this island.
They'll not leave till we're dead;
or until they are well fed!'

'They've found me; I'm finished!
My ammunition has greatly diminished
within the last two days.
From the sea, with the fog, they roll in.
They attack in the haze!'

'My goodness! Golly gosh!
Is that the time? She'll be thinking I'm lost!'

Reading this mad message has lead me astray.
I'll discard this rubbish and get on my way!
That's odd. I don't remember there being a fog warning today.
From the sea, it comes; rolling in, a mist!

'Who's there?'

What's that noise?
What's that hiss?

Philip Trivett

SOLITUDE

Are you my island in the sun,
Have all kinds of life already begun.
I want, it's true, to start anew
My needs are simple, demands are few.
So weave your spell and send for me
A native islander I will be.
A quiet existence is all I seek,
No motorway backlogs from week to week,
No deadlines, or pressure, no stress or strain,
No mental or physical or emotional pain.
The warmth of the sun and a whispering breeze,
Swaying palms, silvery sands, a life I would seize.
But if my whimsical message reached such isolation
Who could return it to this colonised nation?

Maureen Watson

GOD'S MESSAGE

This message has stormed
The mighty sea
A bottle full of memory
For love has struggled
Throughout all time
To nestle in the hearts of man.

A cooling breeze caresses your face
For nothing good does God erase
Love comes in many shapes and forms
But this bottled message comes from God.

Fold it to your heart and know
In spreading His Word you will make love grow
No flotsam jetsom is His Gift
You will feel His love burst into space.

Nothing we ask for does God refuse
If it's for others and this Gift is love
Adios dear friend, whoe'er you may be
Please pass God's Message on for me.

Mary Skelton

MESSAGE IN A BOTTLE

There, up in Ribblesdale, is Stainforth Foss,
Where we went one day to see the fall,
Over rocks so smooth, some covered in moss,
The water gushes over cliff so tall.

I thought of the Ribble and where it would go,
And a plan began to form in my mind,
What if a message was sent down the flow,
On the estuary, someone would find.

So I found me a bottle with tight-fitting top,
And sat down to write a good rhyme.
Then from the top of the fall I did drop,
It survived the fall, and looked fine.

From Settle to Sawley, West Bradford and Mitton,
The little craft sailed, waters fast and some still,
Ribchester bridge, Preston and Lytham,
Till it stopped on a bank across from the mill.

Out went the tide, the mud flats laid bare,
Along came the diggers, searching for bait.
But they didn't see my message sat there,
I guess they'll just have to wait.

I told them how beautiful the Dales were I'd seen,
The colours of autumn, the berries and leaves,
I told them about all the places I'd been,
The majestic hills, and the stream as it weaves.

The beauty of nature, and God's great plan,
It's all told there in the message you see.
At Stainforth, is where it all began,
It's ended at Lytham with sand and the sea.

Joan Jones

MESSAGE IN A BOTTLE

By the time this bottle's floating
Our future hopes lie in the past
What's the point of future planning
When the global die's been cast?

For global warming's hotting up
We watch it with myopic eyes
Mouthing modern solipsisms
In a market place of lies

Thus we live on false pretences
Hardly hiding countless fears
Clinging to our short-term blinkers
Knowing it will end in tears

Do not think we lived so blindly
That we knew not what we did:
Our children's hopes we gobbled up
And all our inner anguish hid

Nicki Cornwell

DISTANT DREAM

There are songs, piano duets,
Concertos I hear with delight
And paintings I see of sunsets;
God blessed me with hearing and sight.
But my loves I choose to condense,
Share with spirit so far unknown
In a world extensive, immense
Where someone like me feels alone.
Artless, adventurous this craft
Wherein resides my yearning plea
Embellished soon by moonlight shaft,
My whim abandoned to the sea.
A fervent call rides here within,
My aspirations ardent, wild,
Heartbeats glassed, gargantuan, spin;
Shall recipient be beguiled?
An enigmatic, winking sun
Tosses its magic far and wide,
Shall not reveal till journey's end
The destiny of words inside.
It seems as though my voice rings far
To comrade of my fantasy
And guided by auspicious star,
I beg you pen reply to me.
I place in this bottle my pride
To chance capricious ocean mood;
Friend, should you find my prayer inside
Read love with which it is imbued.

Ruth Daviat

TROUBLED SEA

Christ Jesus calmed a troubled sea
Many years ago
He will do the same for you
If you ask Him to

Pray to Him with humility and truth
Tell Him all your woe
Then before you finish praying say
Christ Jesus, please come into my life this day

He will come to you
And calm your troubled sea
As He did for me
When I asked Him to

He came to me when I called Him
And took away my woe
So my friend turn to Him and say
Christ Jesus, please come into my life this day.

Simon Barjona

ALL IN THE MIND

Whoever receives this message today,
I hope I have a reply.
I'll tell you what I'm all about,
And the reason why.

I'm tall and slim and very cool,
Strawberry blonde is my colour:
My blue eyes and rosebud mouth,
Will send you all a-flutter.

I'm five times two and eight years old,
A student I am no less.
On the brink of life's adventures,
Don't know the meaning of stress.

Now you wonder why I don't give you,
My name and my present address,
Because these facts are all in the mind,
I wonder - did you guess?

I'm as round as any barrel can be,
My life is all in the past.
I've had my day - I'm seventy-one you see,
Goodness knows how much longer I'll last.

So, if you're a young man and find this bottle,
Don't be all grim and despair.
My grand-daughter Lucy looks like this,
Chin up - there'll be someone out there.

Dorothy Whitehall

NEVER HEARD

I am in need of a penfriend, please write to me,
Read this message, I'm hoping for a reply you see.
My family's spending six months on this island,
There's none my age, I do hope my message is found.
I am in need of friendly written words,
Because although I say a lot, I'm never heard.

Six months on this island will be a tedious task,
Could you answer this note, is it too much to ask!
I'm of the female gender and tall for my age,
I enjoy all sports, favourite colour is beige.
I'd better finish now to catch the evening tide,
And go back up the beach, climb up my tree and hide.

S Mullinger

REGRETS

Jim Croce wanted to put time in a bottle, and I accomplished that fact.
It didn't matter, a bottle, a can or a glass, I drank my life away,
    and that's that!

It was so easy to pour another hour away, buying happiness
    covered with foam.
Now my *regrets* are all piling up, and it's a lonely life that I roam.

One for the road, one for lost love, and one for the courage to dance.
One drunken life now leaves me alone, when I should be
    sharing romance.

It's easy to say I never dropped a drink, but then again,
    how would I know.
God had blessed me with a special blue-green eyed woman to love,
    drunkenly, that did I blow!

My bottle of life floats down the river of time, the message inside
    short and *sad*.
I could have been happy, her love left intact, thus my drunken life
    leaves me, empty and *mad!*

Arlyn Harry Navis

WENDY ISLAND BAY

This message is for you my friend
As time brings fast decay,
It is the last that I shall send
From Wendy Island Bay.

My prayers have lost their constant glow
And dreams go with the tide,
For there's no love to overthrow
This lonesome heart I hide.

When sunrise comes I've cause to weep
As sadness follows me,
And silent shadows seem to sleep
And give no company.

Then I cry out in mental pain
From depths of no rejoice,
Then sadness brings its own refrain
Without a friendly voice.

So by three palms without embrace
My shadow rests today,
And silence now shall take my place
On Wendy Island Bay.

Peter James O'Rourke

THE LEGACY

The year is 9098 and I am celebrating my eighteenth year of life.
I was permitted to walk unchaperoned today, maturity
                                            has its advantages.
Walking along the waterways I noticed a shiny container
                                            half-submerged in the sand.
On reaching home I removed the stopper and shook the vessel,
                                            something fell out,
Unfolding the paper, I saw writing there, I could not
                                            comprehend the words.
I went to see my favourite elder, who is always in the secret
                                            chamber below;
When giving him the paper and the vessel, his eyes lit up
                                            with enthusiasm.
He carefully looked at the writing and told me to return after 2 sunrises.
My excitement was great, what had I found, how old was it?
When I went back, I sat in silence as my grand elder read
                                            the words written there.
He began 'The year was 1999, a man of 35 years was
                                            holidaying in the Bahamas,
His message was a warning, to help people in years to come.
He explained the world was dying, greed prevailing faster
                                            than an express,
He stated that he could speak to anyone in the world in seconds,
Either by phone or electronic mail, he wrote that men were sent
                                            into space regularly,
Medically any organ could be transplanted, limbs sewn back,
                                            wounds healed.
Life expectancy had increased, comforts and aids invented to cut
                                            out mundane chores.
He commented how wars persisted, that violence breeds violence,
A cataclysmic disaster was imminent, Earth was being destroyed,
                                            by deforestation,
The depletion of the ozone layer had changed the weather patterns,
                                            creating havoc,
Storms, like no others ever known, the ice-caps were melting,
                                            the land would disappear.

Chemical warfare was a dark threat, megalomaniacs waiting
                                        to press that button,
Which would kill the world as we know it, please listen, I write this as
                                        a friend, Adam.
I looked at my elder, I truly did not understand, his eyes
                                        were moist, he spoke.
'Adam was right, nuclear weapons created mass destruction in 2038,
Life was annihilated, the planet was in darkness for hundreds of years,
The sun was shrouded in poisonous gasses, creating explosions
                                        that rocked Earth,
Records were found centuries later, I have read their history for years,
They were so clever, so fortunate, but they lost it all;
We are the rebirth, we are primitive, but we must learn from them,
We must never destroy this beautiful planet again, the atmosphere
                                        must remain pure,
The habitation lush, we will never use chemicals, even if we
                                        could create them,
All the documents are a legacy to disaster they must be destroyed'.
He placed the green vessel on the stone, there were raised letters
                                        on its side.
P E R R I E R, I wondered what they signified,
                                obviously something sinister.

Amanda-Lea Manning

MESSAGE IN A BOTTLE 1

If you should find this bottle, contact Sir Cliff Richard,
Please, please ask him to come and rescue me!
I'm trapped in a three-bedroomed semi -
And with him I'd much rather be!
I always seem to be chained to the kitchen sink,
Washing, cooking, cleaning the home,
Instead of living a life of drudgery each day,
With him, I would much rather roam!
I just love his voice and charming manner,
He wouldn't permanently talk about football!
There would be 'no what's for tea, Mum?'
If you find this, *please* give him a call.
Tell him I'll gladly do *his* laundry,
If he will just sing to me!
So, please, if you find this bottle soon,
Call Cliff, before I drift too far out to sea!

June M Bootle

FOR MY LOVE

If this message reaches you
My love with sunrise hair
And shining eyes as lustrous
As the seas of turquoise blue,
You, lithe and graceful
As the running deer, with touch
As soothing as a trickling stream,
Then think of me and know
I did not die.
My longest hours pass by
In thoughts of you
From this strange land
Where neither tongue nor face
Is fitting to my own.
The ebbing tide may bear
This blue and brilliant glass
To reach the one to whom
I vowed my love and long
To see again before I die.
So reader, understand
No meagre word of mine,
No feeble phrase
Does justice to my fairest love.
But I did not forget.

Carol Rickard

THE PARENTS' PRECEDENT

Two million pounds must be found, to pull
Down, and rebuild a comprehensive school,
Because maintenance for it was withdrawn
By one roguish council in Liverpool.

Infuriated parents have now sworn
To set a precedent. They won't re-warn
The council of the damage time has wrought.
Plans for a public suit are being drawn

Up, with their own solicitors, for court.
It is not safe to teach there, or be taught
In science subjects, or home economics -
One day, soon, a fire may have to be fought -

Or left to burn - and make far worse this fix
For careless councillors, who through their tricks
With urban finance, laid off caretakers.
They will not get relief from verbal sticks
Brandished in court by parents, new-ground-breakers.

Gillian C Fisher

MESSAGE IN A BOTTLE

I have no doubt that these words shall be looking out,
They will probably scream, kick and shout.
When the bottle is opened who can tell?
These words may give off an awful smell?
I am hoping that if this should be the fact,
That you will treat them with lots of tact.
For I have no wish that they should offend,
As a returning letter I hope you will send.

Pauline Uprichard

A Bottle Swimming Near

The sea was calm, the sky was blue.
The land looked almost new.
But what could I see, crystal clear?
A bottle swimming near,
Inside the bottle I found a note.

I am an old pirate at sea
And I want to find the key
To unlock the treasure chest
And have a spree!

Emma Freeman

ALL WASHED UP

As I send a bottled poem
To float across the foam
I wonder if an answer
Will come back to me at home.

Will it end up by some palm trees
On a hot and sandy shore
Where the gently moving water
Laps the beach forever more?

Will some dark and dusky maiden
In her colourful sarong
Spot the bottle in the water
As she sings a native song?

I might as well stop dreaming
No palm trees in my reach
The bottle's in a black bag
Washed up on Margate's beach.

So if you want my poem
To put within a book
I'm afraid the local bottle-bank
Is where you'll have to look.

B C Watts

ISLAND 20' 72"

From Island 20' 72"
With longitude and latitude blue,
I've lived a year on fish-head suppers,
These Islanders are complete nutters,

They found me on the sandy shore,
Thought a god had dropped the under score,
So I'm sitting here looking pretty,
While they screech away at a badly tuned ditty,

Please send a boat, I want to go home,
Manchester's calling, I feel alone,
I miss the pubs and late-night fights,
Sparkling canals in the candlelight.

From island 20' 72"
With longitude and latitude blue,
I've lived a year on fish-head suppers,
Please rescue me from these Island nutters.

Fiona Bower

TO WHOEVER

To whoever retrieves this vessel.
I was held hostage by a conflict of emotions,
until I trapped them in this bottle,
then hurled them into the ocean.

From me, their lifeline will be severed.
To you a stranger on the shore,
my tribulations will not invade yours.
Let the sea have them forever more.

Elizabeth Dobie

SEND OUT SUSTENANCE/SOS

This was a good bottle of wine bought for my wife but I just had to
                                                                                                drink it
otherwise when I tossed it into the sea all I'd have done is sink it
Here I am alone on a beach bereft and deserted by my kith and kin
Last thing I can remember, (I was floating and drinking) is seeing a
                                                                                         shark's fin
slicing through the water (I may have been a bit drunk) heading
                                                                                          towards me
I'd had breakfast, a drink or two with my lunch, then the wine, now
                                                                                 I need my tea
or I am afraid I may starve out here - there's not a living soul in sight
I am starting to feel rather cold. What if I have to spend the whole night
laying out under the stars. The sky is darkening and it looks like rain
it's one thing to go swimming when it's sunny but at night I'd prefer
                                                                                          to remain
tucked up warm with my wonderful wife in my cosy king-sized bed
and whatever happens now, in the morning I'm sure to have a sore head
so that if I ever arrive home alive, however I have starved and suffered
I am going to be in very deep trouble - no sympathy will be offered
The first question will be 'Why did you have a bottle with you in the
                                                                                         water?'
I may have imagined the shark but, in reality, there's sure to be
                                                                                 slaughter
There'll not be a thanksgiving service because I'm safe home and dry
there will be a lot of unanswerable questions so that's the reason why
I am putting this note in a bottle for the finder to give to my wife
if she gets this note to say how much I love her it may just save my life
My legs are not reliable enough for me to walk all the way back to my
                                                                                           home
I may have drifted miles down the shore before I waded through
                                                                                  the foam
and finished drinking the wine to remove an alcoholically induced
                                                                                          shark
and now night is coming and I've always been afraid of the dark
so I'll have to stay here until it gets light to find my way back to town

'cause I've lost my sense of direction of which is up the beach and which is down
and I could be walking further from my home in completely the wrong direction
I need a miracle like walking on water or I may need to stage a resurrection.

F B Broomfield

Our Bottled Message

If you're the one who finds our note,
Please send help while we're afloat,
Our radio is on the blink,
And we're afraid that we may sink.

We set sail from Plymouth bay,
On the twenty-first of May,
The year is nineteen eighty-two,
If not too late, please help us do.

A storm has broke our mast apart,
Our engine's stopped and won't restart,
All aboard are low at heart,
The waves may break our boat apart.

Our compass broke the other day,
Where we are I cannot say,
Please radio all ships at sea,
To look for flares sent up by me.

We place our lives in your safe hand,
If it's too late we'll understand,
God bless you if you should try,
We send our thanks in case we die.

G D Eccleston

Hi!

'I'm sending this bottle out to sea
as far as it will go.
The estuary tide is ebbing fast;
winds fan the water's flow.

I'm writing to whoever waits
upon some other shore,
thus hoping to make contact, and
open some foreign door.

So - peace, and love, and freedom, friend;
and if you find my note,
please write to the address above -
I'm sending prayers of hope.'

Then I flung the bottle out to sea,
as far as it would go.
I watched as it sailed away on the tide,
while the winds fanned the ebb and flow . . .

J M Service

MESSAGE IN A BOTTLE

Dear message, in a bottle,
Oh! What a hottle,
How would I escape out of it?
The mind boggles.
But not perplexed!
Oh! Green bottle I wish I,
could
escape out of you!
Because you should write,
your own,
obituary.
But I'm not being morbid,
I give opportunity!
Instead of no way of escape,
Just a sinking ship.
Everyone should have a -
Skipper instead of a kipper!
Then we would all be remembered
and not gone.
Gone with the wind.
But not forgotten.
My own obituary!
Gives a lottle
Therefore I'm not stuck in a bottle.
I'm me, I'm free.

Lynda Margaret Fitch

MESSAGE IN A BOTTLE

Beyond the far horizon . . .
Further than any eye can see,
There is a golden island,
Created in my dreams.

Filled with exotic creatures,
Untouched by the hand of man,
Peace and tranquility in abundance,
Miles of uncharted golden sands.

Surrounded by a smooth glass ocean,
Filled with tall, green-leaved palm trees,
With only one to its population,
That person is *me*.

When sick of the unending rat-race,
Weighed down with burdens of the day,
I climb into my sailboat,
Whispering sea breezes blow me far away.

Over smooth glass oceans,
Towards tall green-leaved palm trees,
As I step onto the golden sands . . .
I find my inner peace.

This is my message in a bottle,
My special island I will share,
When the burdens of life start to get you down . . .
Then you can join me there.

Tracy Bell

Leaving School

As a teenager seeing a future that glows,
I was not an unthinking fool;
So I read my set books and I did my French prose,
Looking forward to leaving school.

Then more broadening vistas of culture arose -
University was the tool,
And I read my set books and I did my French prose,
Still looked forward to leaving school.

Yet to work in this privileged world I then chose
As a lecturer keen and who'll
Go on reading set books and on doing French prose,
Not yet managing to leave school.

As the years passed, this world came to decompose -
Politicians and bureaucrats rule.
Still, I read my set books and I did my French prose,
And I felt for the damage to school.

A demoted profession was now in the throes
Of upheaval and ridicule,
But it lacked enough leaders with will to oppose
Each half-baked and absurd schedule.

And morale and belief fell like sad dominoes;
'Twixt career and good sense, a duel.
Life has more than set books, and much more than French prose:
That's enough, so just go, leave school!

When a system is sick, one can best diagnose
A clear need for change and renewal,
And the taste for intelligent life ever grows
When one finally has left school!

Anne Sanderson

A Reptilian Scene

The jungle's still and dark and wide,
Where lie the snakeys, side by side;
Who dare approach, who dare advance,
To see those eyes convey their trance?
There'll be a price, indeed there will,
To get too close to that head so still;

The head will rise, the neck will snap,
In sinks the fangs, in deep the bite,
The teeth give forth of their vile sap,
And the prey can struggle but lose the fight.
The jungle's still and dark and cruel,
And danger lurks where the snakeys rule.

Alistair McLean

WHISPERS OF THE SEA

'It's time that we were heading home, come Ben, what have you there?
A piece of driftwood, old tin can, please Ben, do bring it here.'

Ben drops his treasure at my feet, tail wags, he sits with grin,
A bottle swathed in seaweed, with something held therein.

How strange, I think, and break the seal to get the paper out,
I wonder where and who it's from, and then let out a shout.

It cannot be from girl I love, but someone with her name,
The writing looks familiar, could it be the same?

I smooth the crumpled paper and sitting on the beach,
'Dear Mark' I read 'I thought I'd write now you are out of reach

I really had to let you go for when you held my hand,
My heart beat fast, I fell in love. I doubt you'll understand.

Now you're back in Australia, it's safe to tell you so,
But since you left I've cried my tears, I thought I'd let you know.

Back here in dear old England, I'm lonely as can be,
I thought I'd write this letter, and give it to the sea.

'Oh Ben, I wonder what to do, it's years since first we met
By now she'll love another, yet her I can't forget.'

I scribble fast with my pen 'I love you, yes, I do
I hope you read this message of my love that's strong and true.'

I cast into Pacific this confession from the shore,
To float inside the bottle to the girl I do adore.

I turn to see Ben running to someone standing near
He barks with glee. 'Darling' she says 'what have you got there?'

'Just a message from a bottle, maybe it is meant to be
The answer to a mystery in whispers of the sea.'

She takes my hand. 'Mark' she says 'on holiday this year,
Could we head for dear old England,
to make sure that she's still there?!'

A Richards

SHE HAD TO GO

For her this life has ended and we are left behind
With a memory of someone who tried to be so kind.

The road of life was sometimes rough just as it has to be,
She took her courage in her hands for everyone to see.

When mantles fell on other lives and darkness hid the day
She'd try to lift the mantle so some light shone on their way.

We're glad she travelled on our road and we would like to share
The love she gave to others by being always there.

Frieda Cox

THE BOTTLE

Menacingly,
It sat upon the table top
It caught my glance, I could not stop,
The bottle glows in the evening light
My body shakes, I cannot fight,
I'm drawn towards its malignant shape
Eyes transfixed, I've no escape.

Love's brought me to this fateful day
The love I had has flown away,
What meaningful reason is left to live
There's no-one else myself to give
Where can I go? What shall I do?
If only I could see life through.

The bottle sits, its cap not open,
To keep it sealed tells thoughts unspoken,
The picture of my love lays scattered
Tormented heart completely shattered,
Decision time has arrived at last
To make an effort to forget the past.

The bottle has gone, the seal unbroken,
Replaced by flowers a romantic token,
Maybe time will heal love's breach
And join as one with harmonious speech
I pray to God this might be true
With all your faults I still love you.

Dusty Sutherland

RETURNED TO SENDER

To the beachcomber, whoever it might be,
who finds this bottled message, sent by sea,
Thinking about it, it is a gamble I suppose,
wondering who will find it, one never knows.

Once it is found, there on that faraway beach,
my message in a bottle, where on earth did it reach,
may be on a desert island, in a far distant land,
and what if the finder, just does not understand.

In with my message, I placed an envelope and stamp,
so I should get a reply, providing the bottle wasn't sank,
It could take many years, before it finds its way to land,
and then it could get lost, on the fast shifting sand.

I must have been lucky, for years later I got a reply,
but sadly when I opened it, I had to have a little cry,
The finders were all Elvis fans, of a Zulu gender,
the only English known to them, was 'Return to Sender'!

Wenn The Penn

A Bottle Of Hope

I am sending this message, through the seas of the world
In a bottle - that will land on some distant shore,
That will tell the finder, of my caged existence
And, hopefully help me - to find an unlocked door.

My name is Abdul Rahmin - I am a student of history
I live at 14 Dronmer St, Tripoli, Libya - an authoritarian state,
Here - the propaganda to the masses, is never-ending
It teaches them to - *hate, hate, hate.*

This hate machine is a steady dose of daily medicine
Fed to the Libyan public - for them to swallow,
But, all this anti-democracy bilge, to me, is nauseating
My conscience tells me - that their words ring hollow.

We Libyans are forbidden to criticise our Colonel
Here - Gadaffi has created a pre-war Fascist state,
On TV, on the radio, in schools and mosques
All broadcast the same message - that Colonel Gadaffi is great.

There is never a mention of the battles of the last war
The heroics of the Desert Rats is forgotten, all is silence,
But - any mention of the USA or Great Britain
Suddenly, the whole media becomes a concerto of violence.

Yes - I would earnestly like to leave my native country
Where so many people have become a flock of sheep,
I would like to emigrate, to any land of freedom
Leaving my native Libya, would be no cause to weep.

But, emigration is only allowed, by having a sponsor
By one who could keep me, in body and soul,
So, please finder, if you can help me to escape
I will repay you, for a free life - that is my goal.

Paul Gold

THE BOTTLED NOTE

To whoever finds this note,
I've had an accident with my boat.
All lives lost and completely alone,
Living on an island all on my own.

Although last week I had a find,
Something that must be one of a kind.
A tribe full of women who want me,
To help them make a family.

Enclosed are jewels which I did find,
They're yours if you act kind,
Of the favour that I ask thee,
Make sure no-one rescues me!

Robert Wassell

MY MESSAGE

I'm stuck on an island,
This message I send,
Help me please,
I'm in need of a friend.

I've put this message,
In a bottle you'll see,
I set it ashore,
And watched it float free.

I'm eating the leaves,
I'm drinking the sea,
Look close and you'll find,
A person called *me!*

Louisa Gibb (13)

ALL WASHED UP!

I sent a message out to sea,
(no, not by radio, or TV)
I wrote, and placed it in a bottle
that I had flung amidst the wattle.
I sealed it up, and threw it wide,
over on the *northern* side,
because I knew the tide would *swirl*,
(I really am a *knowing* girl!) -
and take it many miles away
to come ashore in some small bay.
The message I wrote, so big and clear -
'As you can see, I'm out of beer
as this empty bottle shows -
so now - no drink to drown my woes!
So, if you find this upon the shore,
could you, perhaps, send me some more?'
Then - some time later did I see
a big crate, bobbing on the sea!
I waded out, and brought it in -
'twas full - of *empty* - flasks of gin!
A note, attached, said 'I must write
to say I'm sorry for your plight.
I'm sending bottles by the score
so you can send out notes galore -
and should you need some more, old mate,
I'll send some at a future date.'
I felt as if I *couldn't* win -
I *couldn't* even *smell* the gin!
The sea had washed the bottles clean -
I sat - dreamed of the might-have-been!

Joyce Hockley

TIMELY WARNING

If only thoughts could fly
and, soaring, reach the sky;
the elements transcend;
the laws of nature bend.

I'd send a message there,
through light polluted air.
I'd send an urgent word,
and hope it would be heard.

'Please mark, for your own sake,
our blundering mistake,
and exercise due care
to not pollute your air.'

Grace Mills

Single Lens Reflex

Identity to be, like fog, comes, goes
like snapshot over last twenty-nine years
of Hebridean sun and mist which shows
identity to be, like fog, comes, goes;
had to return to find lost self, loss grows
smaller as courage really forsakes fears;
identity to be, like fog, comes, goes,
like snapshot over last twenty-nine years.

Robert D Shooter

AND!

And!
In the end,
My love for you,
Is love,
I hope you see,
Is true!

Graham Mitchell

MESSAGE IN A BOTTLE

To send out messages in bottles,
is one of the most exciting things to do.
It helps to keep all things in perspective,
And think of the joy you unwittingly give.

One may never have ventured to send one off oneself,
But has found one all the same.
No message is sent seriously,
But does give much joy in the main.

The sender is not really bold,
But the words can warm a heart that is quite cold.
And your mind is kept very active,
As you try to visualise the writer who made those words captive.

Betty Green

A Message To Whomever

To the finder of this bottle, that's floated o'er the ocean blue
Pull the cork and set me free, I'm a message just for you.

Dear sir or madam, I'm writing you this note
For I'm stranded on this island, and sorely need a boat
I need your help so please read on, and I'm sure you'll understand
And decide that you will help me, to escape this cursèd land.

I hope the enclosed diagram will you, my friend, assist
And lead you to this island, through the early morning mist
Latitudes and longitudes are hard to understand
But I hope I've done my very best, in giving you a hand.

So if you're willing my good friend, adventuring to go
Follow my map and search for me
                              signed
                                      Robinson Crusoe.

R J Chapman

MUSHROOM

Mushroom of doom inhabit the coombe,
They are lurking and lingering,
Waiting for rain and damp again,
They spring forth,
Through the soft turf,
Towards the sunlit dew,
Above the grass their heads show waiting,
People are picking and poisoning,
Mushrooms all kinds.

K M Clemo

BOTTLE MESSAGE

Will the person finding this bottle message please be kind enough to forward:-

Miss Sally Albright here, Peter,

You'll be pleased to know I arrived in New Guinea on schedule five years ago, since then had no time to communicate, my life has been hectic trying to make a new life for myself! Still single, couldn't send a letter no Post Office in this area. Please forgive me Peter for this long delay, may this message in the old cider bottle prove fruitful.
The distance and the time has not lessened my love for you, it will last for evermore . . .

To: Mr Peter Askey
12 Warmsley Place
Appleton
Lancs, England.

Alma Montgomery Frank

I MYSELF

To brave the lion in his lair,
What quaking soul his life would dare;
Or twist the tail of crocodile
And seek the lurking tiger's smile?

Who'd ride the waves to distant shores
Where still the golden eagle soars;
And linger with the spouting whales
Till midnight sun the ice-field veils?

Who'd climb the mountain's awesome height
Where glaciers gleam, a fearful sight;
Then tread beside volcano's fire
Where water is the heart's desire?

Not I! I seek the arms of peace
Where all such madness has to cease.
A coward I prefer to be,
Seek refuge in philosophy -
That's me!

Evelyn Balmain

Pandora's Bottle

Ah! So! You opened it then.
Ignored my carefully worded label
Or thought 'Pandora's bottle!' - Just a fable,'
And poked your nose in again.

Do you know what you have done?
The ills and troubles you've just let go?
The weight you've added to this world's woe?
And you thought it just a bit of fun?

Well, now you've got a job to do,
Don't just stand there and gawk.
You've got my bottle, you've got my cork,
Now the rest is up to you.

Are you sure you've left hope free?
Then take my bottle and cork it well,
Contain its unwanted gifts from Hell
And throw it back into the sea.

What?

You forgot about my note, you say?
You dunderhead, you silly ass.
What dreadful things might come to pass
If my bottle's ever found one day.

R L Cooper

SOMEONE SOMEWHERE

Lazing one day by the sea
I got to wondering
Could someone, somewhere, just like me
Be thinking the same thing?
An empty bottle by my side
Prompted the idea,
In it I would place a note
And at the turn of tide
I'd trust my message to the surf
And hope that it would reach
Someone, somewhere, in similar mood
On some far-off beach.
My message very simply said
'To whom it may concern;
When this letter you have read
Please write me by return.
Perhaps a friendship we may forge
If the fates allow,
My home address in Cheddar Gorge
Is printed just below.'
Six months elapsed without a word,
My hopes were fading fast,
Perhaps it all was too absurd
But then one day at last,
A letter dropped upon the mat
In unfamiliar hand,
Delivered by our Postman Pat
'Twas from a foreign land.
My bottle landed seemingly
Far off in the Azores,
The lady who now wrote to me
Had found it on those shores.

Who would have thought that letter brief
Could so change my life,
It really beggars all belief
For now we're man and wife.

Peter Fordham

The Human Race

I send my message out to sea
Across a crowded galaxy
I hope it lands in time to save
My island and its many slaves
The place we live is known as Earth
A planet once full of joy and mirth
But recently most things have altered
Our lives and destinies have faltered
The human race will become extinct
As our world is strangled and forced to shrink
Whoever reads this SOS
Please help us escape from this awful mess.

Chrissi

ALONE IN A BOTTLE

Imagine yourself being placed in a bottle,
And tossed way out to sea,
Not knowing where you will wander,
Or what your life will be.

Surrounded by the ocean,
Only fish for company,
Locked up in a bottle,
Not knowing when you'll be free.

No sign of land approaching,
Just you the sea and the sky,
Laid there in your bottle,
Wishing you were home and dry.

Bobbing up and down on the waves,
Tossed from side to side,
Seagulls pecking at your cork,
Danger but nowhere to hide.

Stormy weather, waves crashing down,
Causing your bottle to swirl round and round,
There you lay head in hand,
Then suddenly bump,
You're back on dry land.

The sand is damp but what do you care,
Pop goes the cork, at last there's fresh air.
Back on land, home and free,
Your journey's been rough,
But you still love the sea.

Sylvia Ranby

MESSAGE IN A BOTTLE

I'm marooned on a desert island
Twixt sun and golden sand
The sea is blue as azure
The air is the purest brand.

I've riches beyond all measure
I've everything I need
I'm in my own blue heaven
I'm in a land of dreams.

I'm in this land of somewhere
And don't know where it is
I'm here on this desert island
I'm here with the man I love.

So please, don't try to find me
Please do not come my way
I'm not in need of saving
I'm here - and I mean to stay.

J Mary Kirkland

IF ANYONE

If anyone does read this message
Please do not throw it away
For it is my only plea
To get rescued some time any day.

If anyone does read this message
Whether near or far away
Spare a thought for me every day
Until you have the chance to fetch me.

If anyone does read this message
Please fetch me with a little boat or plane
I just hope that I can last a long time
And somehow stay sane.

Keith L Powell

THE LOVE BOTTLE

My darling I gaze out to sea from on these clifftops high
Watching for the billowed sails against a darkening sky,
But as I stand here praying for these many weary days
I only see vast emptiness spread far in misty haze.
So I'm sending you this message in a bottle full of love
And hoping that it finds a home within a sheltered cove
Upon a far-off island where maybe you're all alone,
The victim of a shipwreck and that's why you've not come home.
I need you to come back to me and at whatever cost
Because without you pirate mine, I am completely lost.
For riches I will have no more or bales of soft smooth silk
To clothe this maiden's body that you whisper's white as milk.
No lace or ribbons, precious jewels to set my eyes on fire -
So hurry back my darling with my objects of desire!

Paddy Jupp

Around Forever

Here I am,
And there you are,
I'm on the page,
And you're of an age.
I come from afar,
Just like the glistening star,
And wherever I am,
I need not ever fear,
As now you have this,
I can never be missed.

Susan Timmis

What's The Weather Like?

Who and where are you I wonder?
The person and the year I ponder
Here I am in plain old England
A country without pretence
I send this message hence

This is the eve of the millennium
So far we still have peace
But with the insatiable lust for power, weapons and plutonium
Did the race and anger ever cease?

How has technology advanced?
Has it made your lifestyles enhanced?
Today there is a black shadow of terminal disease
With much research to discover a cure
For aids, cancer and many more
Did time cast sunshine and hope?
Only you in the future will know for sure
What I would like to answer now
Where what and how?

Linda J Clarke

SECOND-GLASS POST

Dear friend, Dad took me round the fair
then hired us each a striped deckchair
from near the postcard shop.
I ate some fish and chips for lunch,
bought cheese and onion crisps to munch
then drank my fizzy pop.

I've built a sandcastle and moat,
been sailing on a pleasure boat,
but sicked down my best dress.
Ooh, now a seagull's swooping round . . .
it's dropping splodges on the ground
and making such a mess!

One's bombed down on a man's bald head -
his face is bright fire engine red
with white drips trickling down!
The dribbles look like magic cream,
the one that Mum says is supreme at
tanning white skin brown.

I had a donkey ride, but slipped
and landed in a pile. Mum clipped
me . . . says my sandals smell.
It isn't fair! It's not my fault!
I yelled to make the donkey halt -
it galloped, and I fell!

I'll put this letter I just wrote
inside my pop bottle and float
it miles across the sea.
Oh, *please* write things *you* like to do,
stuff *your* note in a bottle, too,
then sail it back to me!

Maureen Atkin

BOTTLED MESSAGE

Today I launched a message
        upon the storm-tossed sea
In an empty gin bottle,
        and now wait hopefully.

For ten years I've been stranded
        on this Pacific isle
with no one else to talk to
        and it seems quite a while!

I'm dying for a cup of tea
        I'd love some fish and chips,
and each night I lie dreaming
        of a girl's luscious lips.

Now if in time this request
        finds one who'll be my saviour,
Will you do your level best
        to grant me this one favour?

Post haste send me a hamper
        from Harrods a s a p,
filled to the top with goodies,
        and some crumpet - speedily!

Jack Judd

MIND IN A BOTTLE

Perhaps you who find this note,
This message in a bottle,
Are just as inquisitive as I,
Or as imaginative
Visualising who wrote,
And where on earth I lie.

If you a pretty virgin be
Slip into your mind
A handsome image of me,
For presently to find
Your imagination
Can make passionate love you see.

And yet you who are old and grey,
Take comfort in the thought
That I too,
Could be this way
And that inside this glass
Two souls have linked at last.

Across an ocean thought has passed
Riding on those waves so vast
And like a bottle this world is filled,
With messages of hope that thrilled,
But yet inevitably are unfulfilled.

C O Burnell

MESSAGE IN A BOTTLE

'To whom it may concern
   I send this heartfelt little ode:
I really love adventure
   And was tempted to use code

But that would be unfair to you
   (whoever you may be)
So here we go: I'm seventeen
   A shapely five foot three

And I am unattached
   But here's the bit to tease you most
The source of your frustration lives
   Two miles along the coast!'

Brian Willis

MY MESSAGE IN A BOTTLE

Whoever finds this message
I hope they'll make great haste
And pass it onto someone who can
Help me win a race.

The race that I'm describing
Is not just one for fun
It could save many people
So please hurry everyone.

I'm stranded on this island here
And don't know where I am
That's why I've sketched a map of it
As neatly as I can.

The inhabitants are hostile here
And high above us all
A landslide has just started
Which is bound to kill us all.

So could you send an aeroplane
It's sure to help us too
As long as it can find us all
Before the day is through.

I'm going to throw my bottle now,
But just before I do
I'll kiss it first, as then with luck
It may wash up near you.

Merilyn Gulley

Help

The last of the wine
was really quite fine
and now that it's through
I'm writing to you

I think we should meet
for something to eat
and if you would pay
that would make my day

I think I'll order steak, then ice-cream
Oh no, I'm awake, it was only a dream
so I'll throw this bottle into the sea
and I hope you get this message from me.

Joy Benford

FREEDOM!

I write this, to you my love,
'Bout all our years of bliss,
As I sit here all alone,
With all my memories!

Tell 'pissed-up Pete', I miss him so,
And also 'Jack-the-lad',
Neighbour Nigel's fondly missed,
Sincere regards to dad!

I hope our boy is doing well,
No doubt at university,
Jane must have had her baby now!
Another mouth to feed.

I'll have to waterproof my roof,
The rain is pouring in,
I shiver slightly, in the cold,
My life has come to this!

I've found the joys of nature,
Compared to city life!
It's really not so bad,
And sometimes rather nice!

No more boss to serve!
No more bills to pay!
Listen carefully, my love!
I think I'd rather stay!

Dancer

TITANIC

It all happened so many years ago,
I still hear distant cries
I was cold that night, it was bitterly cold
I was getting very sleepy
As it was my maiden voyage
The scenes were spectacular
I was being called ruler of the sea.

I was as proud as I could be
I was shiny, clean and most of all immortal
The Titanic was described as tantalising
I sailed for five long hard days
It was tough but I knew I would make it
People were sleepy, it was like they had been drugged.

Then I felt a bump on one side
It felt like I was getting heavier
It felt like I couldn't breathe, I was drowning
I thought I was immortal, but it was not to be
My God, my family.

Now I'm at the bottom of the sea
Decades have passed with me thinking about family
When I had wished I had reached my destiny.

Sunny Gunessee (13)

SHIPWRECKED

Hello! This message is from me,
I was shipwrecked on an island
In the South Seas.
There's very little to do all day,
No hard work but plenty of time to drink rum,
Romance the dancing girls and play.
The days are hot and the nights are sweet,
There's plenty to drink
And plenty to eat.
The reason why I did not state my name,
Is because I do not want to be rescued.
I want to stay!

Robert McCall

MESSAGE IN A BOTTLE

When you get this
Please make it clear
That it came from afar and not near.
The smudged date is right
As it was cast overboard at night,
In a fit of pure rage
Did my tears fall upon the page.
He's run off with another,
Leaving us behind,
Dog, cat, newborn humankind
Wife and mother.
Tell him and others wherever they may be
It's wrong to cause such anguish
To ones as weak and trusting as we.
So in faith to set our tortured souls free
Like Ophelia I've cast us all into the sea.

Helena Edwards Bishop

RSVP

OK you guys . . . it's *nostalgia* time . . .
Let me take you back . . . back to 1979,
when punk was dead, and flares went 'out'
the first time round. Will you find this note in 1999?
It is summer . . . I am on holiday in Brighton . . . so very young.
Tubeway Army are still at number one. 'Are Friends Electric?'
I hope so. By the time you read this, I may have fizzled out,
or got really old like my mum who wears slippers with
pom-poms on and mimes with a comb in the mirror to The Beatles'
'Twist and Shout' . . . I'd rather be dead than like that.
'Message in a Bottle' . . . Do you remember the words?
'Just a castaway . . . No-one here but me - Oh . . .' How does it
sound in 1999? . . . 'I'll send an SOS to the world . . .' Do you
even remember The Police? They are chocolate right now. I
suppose they will be old, fat and grey by then . . . 'More loneliness
any man can bear - oh' And by the way, do you still have
records? You know, the black vinyl stuff? I doubt it. The reason
I am writing this is because I'm so lonely . . . 'Love can mend your
life, but love can break your heart . . .' So if you care, please
reply. 'I hope that someone gets my message in a bottle . . .
Yeah.'

Barbara L Richards

MESSAGE IN A BOTTLE

To the discerning female
who uncorks this quaint bottled verse,
guided by moon current and gale,
swallowed by 'fin-backs' or worse.

Spare kind thoughts for the fellow
whose clothes are all falling apart,
and, with teeth turning quite yellow,
claims you the salve for his heart.

Do not revile nor deride
in view of his lack of 'station',
it's not the seen, but what's inside
is due one's adulation.

If he needs light, give a lamp,
but if for such love you don't care,
remember - where you see a tramp -
might be a millionaire.

Phoenix Martin

SEAWORTHY?

Wild waves lash the pebbled shore.
Night winds begin to howl.
Dogs wake from their twitchy sleep,
No cat is on the prowl.

I walk beside the raging sea,
Swept forward by the storm.
Each footfall's one step further from
The safe, the know. The warm.

I've got with me two bottles.
One, pills. The other, booze.
(When I lost you, I lost it all.
There's no more left to lose.)

I know you're out there somewhere
Sailing aimlessly,
In search of new enchantresses,
A thousand miles from me.

I drink the whisky bottle dry
And sink down on my knees,
Screaming to the ravaged sky
'Forgive me, lover. Please.'

A notepad's in my pocket,
Pen through its spiralled side.
I scrawl these words, and bottle them
Hurl to the foaming tide.

And darling, when this reaches you,
If Neptune's feeling kind,
You'll see me swimming for my life
Not very far behind . . .

Elizabeth Mark

SONNET: BRIGHT EYES BURNING LIKE FIRE

Soft cuddly fur and friendly twitching nose,
Long silken ears and clear bright eyes like those
Were never meant for tears. Oh how can we
Subject them to such inhumanity?
How can we with cold-blooded callous ease,
Force eyelids back and wilfully release,
Drop after drop of liquid agony,
Into those trusting eyes so heartlessly.
To smart, to sting, to burn and even blind
And swear it's for the good of all mankind.
How can we treat God's creatures in this way
Then go to church to proudly sing and pray?
What hypocrites we are, both you and I,
Not to see God within a rabbit's eye!

J D Winchester

LISTEN!

Life is a story in volumes of three,
the past, the present, and yet to be.
The past we have read and put away,
the present we live from day to day.
The future we are not allowed to see,
for God, alone, keeps the key.

Beings are born, just to grow old;
some are gentle, some are bold.
There are good, there are bad.
Life can be happy, also sad.
It is a gamble of struggled and strife,
but take what comes and smile through life.

Live your life sensibly;
don't delve into a future, which you are not meant to see!

Annemarie Poole

MESSAGE IN A BOTTLE

Hello my friend, my new-found friend,
I'm glad you've found my note.
Despatched in this glass envelope,
How long was it afloat?
Not stamped, addressed or letter-boxed,
But carried on the tide,
Drifting all the way to you,
My letter safe inside.
You'll see that I have dated it
And put my address too,
In the hope that one day soon
I would hear from you.
I have so many questions that
I don't know where to start.
Who are you, and where are you?
How far are we apart?
How did you come to find my note?
Was it close to hand?
Floating just within your reach
Or washed up on the sand?
Please write back and we may be
Pen pals evermore,
But send it via the postman as
It's quicker door to door!
I'll bring this little letter to
An optimistic end,
And say goodbye for now, from me,
To you, my new-found friend.

F Jensen

GUILTY

What have we done to this England so fair
Have we the nerve to explain
Should we be making our children aware
Of what we destroyed for our gain?

The fish in our seas have almost run out
but we were too greedy to heed
The warnings of those who knew without doubt
To where all this madness would lead.

Fields of old England, a sight to be seen
The wide open spaces we knew
Mile after mile of incredible green
Now tarmac hides most from our view.

We ripped out the hedgerows, without a thought
Of wildlife that live in its shade
Prairie-like fields was the object we sought
And nobody bothered who paid.

Coal and oil stocks are exceedingly low
We still use them both with aplomb
Fouling the air and the seas as we go
The environmental time bomb.

Billions of people have lived on this land
But none more destructive than we
Our self-centred ways will be writ in the sands
'The vandals of this century'.

Bob Wydell

OUT OF REACH

I slung this off of Clacton Beach
For my flat was out of reach,
I send it across the miles
To bring to you tons of smiles.
If you would like to answer
Don't expect no fancy dancer.
Just a normal English chap
In his coat and flat cap.

I picked a bottle of Special Brew
To send my message off to you,
As it floated on the wave
I hope it reaches you before the grave.
You are far off I am told,
But each day I am getting old.
Too young for death, too old for sex,
From a kind chap in old Essex.

Colin Allsop

To Who It May Concern

To who it may
Concern
For we all
Would like to
Learn
Where this
Message shall
End
Whose thought
Anybody could ever
Send
When they
Do not know
The name of the
Finder
Many years from
Now

Coleen Bradshaw

A World Alone

If you find these words
Know that I was here,
A being on this earth
Drinking the air,
Shouting to the sky -
Know that I was there.

Where the sands of time
Sift and dune,
And where I walk,
My footsteps sleeping
In the yellow crystals
Silently disappearing.

Where white sails unfurl
Against azure sky,
On cliff and shore
Washed by restless seas,
Know I am here
In the salt breeze.

My ship sails on
So seek not to find me,
But know I am here,
Know I'm at one
On this rock-hewn isle
With a world alone.

Esme Francis

A Message In A Bottle

Somewhere, out there, a kindred spirit like me
Yearns for contact across the sea.
Will a message in a bottle make that link
Or will fate determine that it shall sink?
Shall my message be witty and terse
Or act as a vehicle for my romantic verse?
It matters not to me the form it takes
As long as a successful journey it makes.
It may be weeks, months or years afloat,
Unnoticed by birds, fish or people in boats.
Yet unconcerned it will bob and dip
And in a storm may even manage a little flip.
In all probability it will not achieve its goal
And will remain unread by any living soul.
Yet the remote gamble that it could create a liaison
Will ensure my message in a bottle journeys forth regardless of reason.

A Jessop

I Wonder

Hello, to someone in a far-off place
We don't know each other, I've not seen your face
The message's in English, can you understand
What is your name, where is your land

I've often wondered who's out there you see
With a wife and two children, happy like me
Not all the world wants fighting and war
We'd rather be friendly, have peace evermore

Buenos dies, bonjour, just hello
We're very far north, are you below
Are you a reader, a writer or such
Could you reply, if so, thank you so much

I married my wife a long time ago
You can't love a person you, don't even know
We didn't meet 'foreigners' back in those days
I always regretted those limiting ways

As an industrial nation we have fax and phones
Power and fuel, but still everyone moans
Maybe you're luckier on your island
Where the sun shines bright, and nothing is planned

Please find a way, translate if you can
Get to a fax/phone and we'll make a plan
If you can't read, a meet-up looks bleak
Let's hope you re-float it, and the bottle don't leak

The Earth is spherical, and rotates once a day
Two-thirds is water, and you're far away
The British Isles are a speck on the chart
This bottle's been lucky, or fate gave it heart

B M Hurll

MESSAGE IN A BOTTLE

Within a bottle oh so blue
I placed a letter just for you
There were so many things to say
You though are so far away
It told of things so long ago
The life we built, then let go
Laughter on the day we wed
Confetti falling near the bed
Children coming, we had four
A key to open our front door
Those years flew fast
Love did not last
Once more I went through that door
The key now was mine no more
Time now has shown me clear
Those things that cost us dear
We did not share the values
Give time to keep love new
Four walls became my shell
Your name was on the bell
My restless heart took me away
Far from home and you one day
I travelled on a stormy tide
My eyes were closed, something had died
Today I put words and feelings
In this bottle, then kneeling
Sent it to you upon the water
White horses tossed it, did I hear your laughter?

Elizabeth Cowley Guscott

TO A STRANGER

When you open this bottle, whoever you are
This message comes from my heart
Read carefully stranger be you near or afar
Beware of the things I impart

We live in a time of few saints
Surrounded by famine, flood, war
Day after day bad and worse news
Wondering what it's all for

Why didn't we try to follow the rules
We were taught when small and green
There are not enough of us trying for peace
We don't care what hell others have seen

Look at the beauty of the Earth
Open your eyes to the world
Help someone helpless show them your worth
Your soul will be unfurled

If you did just that to your neighbour
Follow the very first law
Open your arms to ease their labour
You will know what love is for

We can make this world sweet and pure
We can make it all worthwhile
Remember these words from a bottle stranger
Before we forget to smile.

Joyce Pompei

BEFORE WORDS

There is something
which was before Time was,
or there were words to tell it.

And Man
found that he could speak
and project words
framed by his mouth,
and that he could multiply words
beyond numbering;
and use them
> to strengthen and sustain;
> to exaggerate and explain;
> to coax, convince, and complain;
> to complicate, dominate, enslave, or entertain -

all to his own advantage!

And the something
which pre-dated time and words
was lost.

But sometimes
in the still night's silences
the Spirit tries to recall
what the Soul once knew.

But Man
can only comprehend
what may be expressed
in a surging torrent of words
which engulfs
the Truth he knew
before Time was
and before words were!

Dan Pugh

MESSAGE IN A BOTTLE

This simple bottle in the sand
Was posted in the sea.
To someone who will understand
The message sent by me,

It may be such a tiny thing
A greeting, or a card,
A poem, or some mundane thing,
Like money, times are hard

Or just the hand of friendship,
Family details, or the like
Or seeking new employment,
Like the phrase 'Get on your bike,'

To find some new adventure,
Far away, across the foam,
In a land of opportunity,
Thousands of miles from home.

Perhaps suggesting marriage,
Or a partnership of sharing,
Proposing life together
In an ecstasy of caring

A vague or hopeful message
That may never find its mark.
Illuminate some memory,
To lighten up life's dark.

Buffeted by wind and rain
To reach its journey's end.
Will it be lost on jagged rock
Or picked up by a friend?

This fragile messenger of glass
Corked tight against the sea.
Hopefully will find that friend
Who'll maybe contact me . . .

Leonard Coleman

A Wish Within

Into a little bottle, stuff a scrawled note,
A wish within,
Hurl it into the sea to float.

To bob about like a little lifeboat,
Over waves, the bottle with wish within
Into a little bottle, stuff a scrawled note.

A wish on the note,
To fully understand the world we live in,
Hurl it into the sea to float.

A simple wish, a prayer of hope,
For the poor, the weak and the starving,
Into a little bottle, stuff a scrawled note.

A wish for these who cannot cope,
Through their difficulties win,
Hurl it into the sea to float.

From the heart a wish of hope,
Food for the starving,
Into a little bottle, stuff a scrawled note,
Hurl it into the sea to float.

B G Clarke

THE LAST RESORT

There is a holiday resort
In Spain that's very new;
This place is so expensive that
All I can say is, 'Phew!'

The hotels are exclusive -
Golf and tennis is the racket;
So that must be why this resort
Is known as Costa Packet!

The rain in Spain falls mainly
On the plain, or so I've heard.
I think this is a pack of lies -
Yes, really, every word:

The weather's awful on this beach;
There's hail, and thunder's near.
My hotel's lousy, food is bad,
PS Wish you were here . . .
(. . . instead of me!)

Roger Williams

RIVER

Carry me to the sea old man
Past your riverbanks, and trees.
Show me the oceans, that I long to see,
Let me know, what it's like to be free.

Show me the oceans that roam the world,
Let me bask in the waves of the sea.
Take me to those tropical isles,
Let me feel in my bones that I'm free.

I can float like a cork, on the ocean waves,
Be tossed about by the seas.
Out there on the waves where the albatross flies,
That's when I know that I'm free.

Oh! river, flowing past my door,
Please carry this message for me.
Let no barrier stop your speed,
Flow quickly to the seas.

Please tell them of my dreams,
The oceans and the seas.
Tell them of my dearest wish,
And how I long to be free.

K J Seeley

BOTTLE-CHART OMISSION

At Leigh, in Essex I was propelled at high tide,
Amid glee, into the sea from the quayside,
Water-tight bottle, dull message inside
To be blown by wind and wave to travel far, oceanwide.

The note read, 'If you find me please hurry to write
And tell by whom, where, when, time of day or night!'
I ask you! Forced into gruelling plight
To please a tipsy party-goer's whim and fancy-flight!

Launched, I submerged, regurgitated, thankfully,
Due to kindness, shown by Thames estuary,
Heading for the Channel or the North Sea?
Treated like flotsam! Me! That once enclosed finest brandy!

Floated, bounced, bobbed and glided gracefully along,
Thrust, pushed, tossed as bad weather blew up strong;
What pressure! Jettisoned! Once had elan!
My foisted voyage taken toll, chip acquired to last lifelong.

Lurched roughly in squally gusts on surf-rolling wave,
Wallowed beneath explosive cavernous nave,
Turmoiling water, held fast as a slave,
Fought and battled to the surface from a Davy Jones' grave.

Ridden atop foaming white caps and white horses,
Wafted onward with gentle cat's-paw sources,
Companionably named, no discourses
Regarding avoidance perilous shipping-lane courses.

Caught in cross-currents and trapped in Indian lunghi,
Dropped overboard from overloaded ferry,
Soon sank without trace, but fortunately,
Minutes before I extricated myself adeptly.

Beached on an island; now I'm proudly on display;
The joke being, no name or address penned on my fateful day!

Hilary Jill Robson

TRICKY TREASURE

Hello, at last you've found me,
Floating in the sea.
I am a little letter,
Which could make your life much better!
I know of buried treasure,
In one huge, enormous measure.
X does mark the spot,
Where this treasure can be got.
A spade will come in handy,
As this place is very sandy!
You'll need water and a jeep,
For the Sahara sand is deep!
I don't know the exact position,
But to find it is your mission.
And when you find that buried gold,
Please don't forget who it was that told!

C Shadwell

MESSAGE IN A BOTTLE

This is my very last desperate plan
A note in a bottle put into the sea
I am thirty plus and still have no man
Can you imagine what that means to me?

I hope it will float for a long, long way
To be found by someone at the edge of a bay,
Gently pushed up by a rising tide
With that precious note still safe inside.

Let a handsome man be the first to see
That special message that was written by me.
Here's hoping he'll read what is said in there
And write to save me from dark despair.

I put in a photo as well as the letter
And begged him to answer to make me feel better
What a wonderful thing if we met one day
And after a while he decided to stay.

Perhaps wedding bells will ring out one day
Then all my unhappiness would fly away.

Renie Calcraft

PLEASE LISTEN

Please listen to what I say,
don't only hear my voice.
My words are important for your ear,
if you would only understand my noise.

Please listen to what I mean,
when I tell you how I feel.
Don't impose your thoughts over mine,
and infer my fears are not real.

Please listen to me when I cry
my feelings out to your heart.
Or turn away, or even try
to talk to others when I start.

Please listen to my language,
when I open my arms to you.
I ask for help to salvage,
my life, so I can start anew.

Joan Lister

MESSAGE IN A BOTTLE

I am a lonely, shy, young woman,
Looking for a friend,
Who'll understand the way I feel,
So I this message send.

The sun glints on my bottle
As it floats upon the waves,
Perhaps my heart on some far shore,
Will find the love it craves.

There must be many people,
Alone and sad like me,
Who cannot find the words to tell
They need some company.

Now I've a dream to cling to
As my hopes float far away,
And an answer may one day return,
Adrift the salt sea spray.

Elaine Beresford

Message Of Hope

The bottle bobs now on the waves, slowly out of sight,
Will it reach another land its message sealed up tight,
The seas around our native isle may see the ebb and flow,
A tiny speck this bottle is, our thoughts now with it go.

Its message speaks of charity, of peace, with no more war,
It carries with it hope and joy as it travels far,
The love of mankind worldwide now precious indeed,
Sowing the seeds of happiness, goodwill without greed.

It may drift at last to reach a distant shore,
In hope that countries may live in harmony evermore,
So man can be like brothers ever now worldwide,
Striving for what is good, standing side by side.

Washed by mighty oceans and many foamy seas,
The message in a bottle tries so hard to please,
To spread the word and tell the truth now it's given scope,
And give some far-off people just a little hope.

Alister H Thomson

GREEN, OPAQUE AND TANTALISING

Quaintly shaped,
Harsh edges smoothed by endless waves,
It lay, undamaged
Beneath the cliff.

Years on, I estimated,
Corkless, quite empty.
Names, identity
Washed clean away.

Far too valuable a find
To throw back into the sea.

Imagination curled round its lip,
A voice - faint and slightly foreign
Slipped and slopped inside.

'You've found me,
Oh, how long I've waited for you.
Take me home, gently,
Cradle me carefully,
Place me alongside your other treasures.

Perhaps it wasn't a fantasy,
The bottle moved slightly
Beneath my hands
And then lay still.

Home is the wanderer,
Home from the sea.

Safe, on my shelf.
When I am very still
I hear its voice
Talking to me.

Helen Perry

BEACHED BOTTLES

Cool beer, it whispered
From the tap
Enticing him away
From life as for so long
He'd known it
Routine day-to-day

Shapely bottles
Flaunted wares
He was too weak to run
From one small sip
At paradise
Reality's no fun

The spirit
Of adventure
Gripped him
Forced the man to drink
And deep into the quagmire
His life began to sink

Sweet fruity wines
With promises
Caressed him for a while
But how soon the drink turned sour
He'd found its grimace
Lost its smile

Kim Montia

WAVES OF CHANGE

In my bottle would be a message
As warm and soft as a fleece
A call for universal all-time peace

Let all fear and hatred be gone
And love with harmony come to stay
No more construction of things that kill
But a higher use of every skill.

The world would be truly one-place
With happiness and a smile on every face
Each would help the other to grow
From many hands of sun and snow

What a happy place the world would be
If answered the message from the bottle at sea.

Clive Cornwall

A Forethought

Why didn't I think of it before, rejection
slips from Editors of my exciting news.
My seafaring message has set me free,
No expert's choice, oh shall I obey the rules,
avoid the hurt and rude.
I am sitting here on a natural shore by the Aegean,
recovering from drinking my very last bottle of gin.
'Oh my head'.
Here is the message and the slips -
This time I swear 'Never again,' I hope to recover.
I do not need it, happier and work better without it.
'Oh I must tell you I just fell in love with a recovering lush,'
A handsome brute that's ageing.
We both must keep the mind and body healthy
so we can mate like mice, not much breeding in this
ageing lady sitting here by the Aegean.

Margaret Gleeson Spanos

ENIGMA

If you find this message true
Don't think that it's meant for you,
For though you have the note in hand
Its destination wasn't planned.

Yet you might say that synchronicity
Knows its own, sublime simplicity,
And that fate is meant to be,
And that is why you heard from me.

And if that destiny perchance
Has brought my note within your glance,
It's just to tell you I'm going away,
So don't come and look for me after today.

But this enigmatic note will be
Always in your memory.

Linda Anne Landers

SEND SOMEONE PLEASE

This is a message
An SOS
To anyone out there
I'm in a mess

I've been stuck in this place
For a hundred and ten days
I've gone round and round
And round this maze

There's no way off
This island of trees
I need a ship
To take me over the seas

To save me from
This lonely place
I need someone now
For my sunburnt face

Help me please
If you can
My name is Crusoe
Yes, I'm that man!

Maxine Beck

FROM BANDOS ISLAND

Palms laced with frangipan
Hide coral strand
Coconuts carelessly
Crash onto sand
Hermit crabs shop for shell
By mangrove root
At night giant bats glide out
Hunting for fruit.

Sue Knight

SUBMISSIONS INVITED
SOMETHING FOR EVERYONE

POETRY NOW '99 - Any subject, any style, any time.

WOMENSWORDS '99 - Strictly women, have your say the female way!

STRONGWORDS '99 - Warning! Age restriction, must be between 16-24, opinionated and have strong views. (Not for the faint-hearted)

All poems no longer than 30 lines. Always welcome! No fee! Cash Prizes to be won!

Mark your envelope (eg *Poetry Now)* **'99**
Send to:
Forward Press Ltd
Remus House, Coltsfoot Drive,
Peterborough PE2 9JX

OVER £10,000 POETRY PRIZES TO BE WON!

Judging will take place in October 1999